萬里長城

Customs, Traditions and Landmarks |
Non-Fiction Series

Copyright © 2022 by Level Learning, INC. and Washington Yu Ying PCS™
Original and Edited Text Copyright © 2022 by Washington Yu Ying PCS™

All rights reserved. No part of this book in whole or part may be reproduced without written permission from the publisher.

Published by Level Learning, INC.
Content Contributors:
Washington Yu Ying PCS™
Level Learning - Ya-Ching Chang

Illustrations by: Matt Austin

Leveling classification based on Level Learning standard. For full description, visit www.levellearning.com

ISBN 978-1-64040-033-7
Traditional Chinese Edition

About Level Learning:

Level Learning provides a literacy focused curriculum specifically designed for K-12 Chinese as a Second Language classrooms. Our program offers 20 levels of specific and detailed objectives, leveled texts and passages, mastery-based online assessment, and analytics to enable data-driven instruction. Level Learning reading curriculum for both literature and informational text emphasize grammar and comprehension skills to help teachers develop confident and independent Chinese language readers. The non-fiction series of books are specifically designed to support our informational text course based on multiple national standards. To learn more about our entire offering, visit www.levellearning.com.

About Washington Yu Ying PCS™:

Washington Yu Ying PCS is a Mandarin English dual language immersion International Baccalaureate (IB) World school. Yu Ying's mission is to inspire and prepare young people to create a better world by challenging them to reach their full potential in a nurturing Chinese/English educational environment. Yu Ying's comprehensive IB, dual immersion curriculum equips students with global competencies for success in the real world. As a leader in immersion education, Yu Ying is determined to advance Chinese language programs and global citizenry education by helping other schools create and strengthen their Chinese programs. For more information, email: products@washingtonyuying.org

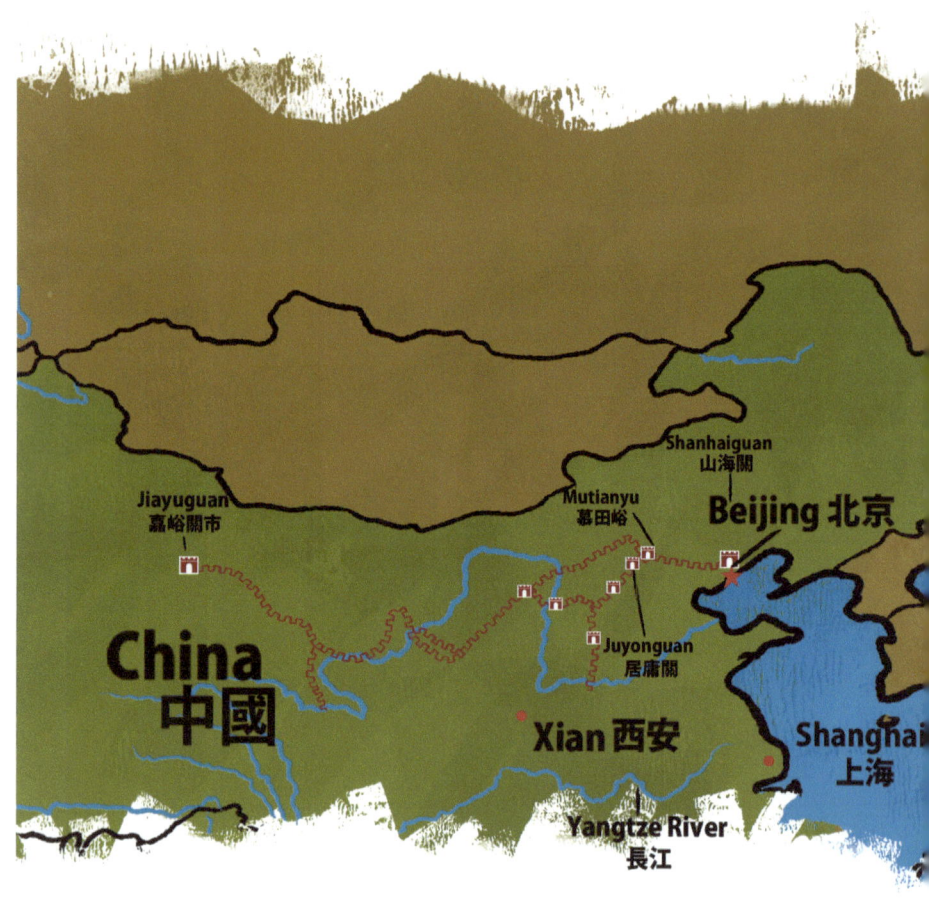

很多人都說,去中國旅行一定要去長城。因為長城不僅是一個著名的景點,而且也是中國最偉大的建築之一。長城在中國的北方,有8851公里長,因此又被稱為「萬里長城」。

長城已經有兩千多年的歷史了。在中國歷史上，很多朝代都修建過長城。雖然秦始皇不是第一個下令修建長城的君王，但是只要說到長城，人們一定會先想到秦始皇，因為他對長城的修建有非常大的影響。

在秦朝時期，一些北方的民族經常南下搶東西。後來，秦始皇下令把一些北方原有的城牆連接起來，用來保護北方的人民。有了這道長城，那些北方的民族就很難再南下，南方的人民就也可以更安心地生活了。

可是在兩千多年前，修建長城並不是一件簡單的工作，需要很多人力和物力。所以秦始皇下令讓一百多萬人去北方修建長城。修建長城的工作不僅辛苦，而且北方的天氣也非常寒冷。在修建長城的這段時間，很多人因為生病或受傷而死在長城下。

修建好的長城,每隔一段距離就有一個烽火台。當烽火台上的士兵看見遠方有軍隊靠近時,白天他們就會在烽火台上點煙,晚上就會點火。其他烽火台上的士兵看到了,就知道要準備保護國家了。

在**明朝**時期，長城又被重新修建和加長。我們現在看到的萬里長城，大多是在明朝的時候修建的。

中國有一句話是「不到長城非好漢」,所以很多遊客都會去登長城,做好漢。不只是中國人,也有很多外國人到中國登長城。很多外國人認為沒有登過長城,就好像沒有去過中國。

你登過長城嗎?有機會也去登長城,做好漢吧!

Glossary

	Pinyin	English Definition
旅行	lǚ xíng	to travel
長城	cháng chéng	the Great Wall
景點	jǐng diǎn	scenic spot
建築	jiàn zhù	building
北方	běi fāng	north
公里	gōng lǐ	kilometer
萬	wàn	ten thousand
里	lǐ	a Chinese unit of length (one li is ½ kilometer)
兩千	liǎng qiān	two thousand
歷史	lì shǐ	history
朝代	cháo dài	dynasty
修建	xiū jiàn	to construct
秦始皇	qín shǐ huáng	The first Emperor of the Qin Dynasty
下令	xià lìng	to order
君王	jūn wáng	emperor

	Pinyin	English Definition
影響	yǐng xiǎng	influence
民族	mín zú	ethnic people
經常	jīng cháng	often
南下	nán xià	to go south
搶	qiǎng	to grab
牆	qiáng	wall
連接	lián jiē	to connect
保護	bǎo hù	to protect
難	nán	hard, difficult
安心	ān xīn	peace of mind
簡單	jiǎn dān	simple
人力	rén lì	manpower
物力	wù lì	physical resources
一百多萬	yì bǎi duō wàn	more than a million
辛苦	xīn kǔ	hard, exhausting
寒冷	hán lěng	cold

	Pinyin	English Definition
受傷	shòu shāng	injury
死	sǐ	to die
隔	gé	separated
距離	jù lí	distance
烽火台	fēng huǒ tái	beacon tower
士兵	shì bīng	soldier
遠方	yuǎn fāng	far away
軍隊	jūn duì	army
靠近	kào jìn	close by, near
煙	yān	smoke
準備	zhǔn bèi	to get ready, to prepare
明朝	míng cháo	Ming Dynasty
好漢	hǎo hàn	hero, strong and courageous person
遊客	yóu kè	tourist
登	dēng	to climb

www.ingramcontent.com/pod-product-compliance
Lightning Source LLC
Chambersburg PA
CBHW041223070526
44584CB00001B/75